Marvellous Maths
Numbers

By David L. Stienecker

Illustrations by Richard Maccabe

CHERRYTREE BOOKS

A Cherrytree Book

Adapted by A S Publishing from
Discovering Math
First published by Benchmark Books
Copyright © Marshall Cavendish Corporation 1996
Series created by Blackbirch Graphics Inc
Series editor: Tanya Lee Stone

This edition first published in 1997
by Cherrytree Press Ltd
a subsidiary of
The Chivers Company Ltd
Windsor Bridge Road
Bath BA2 3AX

British Library Cataloguing in Publication Data
Stienecker, David L.
    Numbers
    1. Arithmetic—Juvenile literature 2. Arithmetic—Problems,
exercises, etc.—Juvenile literature
    I. Title
    372.7'2

ISBN 0 7451 5314 3

Printed and bound in the USA

Contents

Numbers Past and Present

When we write numbers, we use a symbol for each number instead of writing the word.

word	one	two	three	four	five	six	seven	eight	nine
symbol	1	2	3	4	5	6	7	8	9

Many ancient civilizations had their own symbols for numbers. Here are a few:

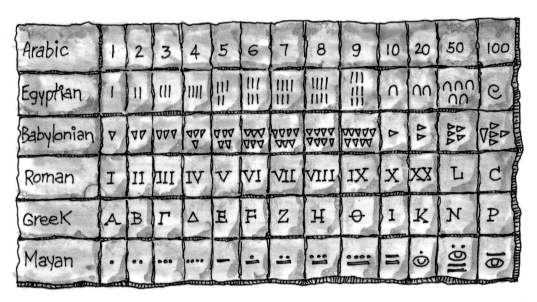

Look carefully at the chart. One row of number symbols should look familiar. Which one is it?

That's right! The number symbols we use today are called Arabic numbers. Arab traders began introducing the symbols to the Western world about 1,200 years ago. But the Arabs didn't make up the symbols. They borrowed them from the Hindu people of India.

Look at the chart again. What other number system looks familiar? Is it the Roman numbers? We usually refer to them as numerals. You have probably seen Roman numerals on old inscriptions and on clock faces.

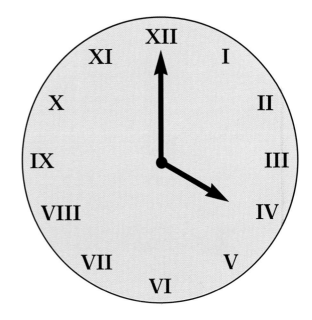

• Trace the clock on a piece of paper and then write the Arabic numbers for the Roman numerals on the clock face.

• Which two numbers are the hands of the clock pointing to?

• What time does the clock show?

Now write down what these numbers are in the Arabic system. Use the chart of number symbols to help you work them out.

Number Shapes

You can show the shape of the number 6 this way.

More than 2,500 years ago, the ancient Greeks thought that the shape of a number had magic powers.

They called numbers that could be arranged in a triangle, triangular numbers.

• Use some coins or other objects to show the triangular shape of the number 6. Then add another row to your triangle. Count the number of coins. What is the next triangular number?

• Now take two rows away. What triangular number do you have now?

This chart shows how to find triangular numbers by looking at number patterns.

• What patterns do you see between triangular numbers?

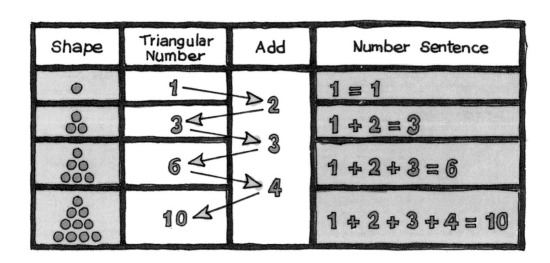

Shape	Triangular Number	Add	Number Sentence
○	1	2	1 = 1
○○	3	3	1 + 2 = 3
○○○	6	4	1 + 2 + 3 = 6
○○○○	10		1 + 2 + 3 + 4 = 10

• There are fifteen triangular numbers between 1 and 120. See if you can work them out. Try using number patterns. If you aren't sure of a number, see if you can show it as a triangle.

Here's another shape the Greeks made with certain numbers. What number does this shape show? What shape does it make?

• Use some coins or other objects to show the square shape of the number 9. Then add enough coins to make the next largest square. What square number does it show?

The Greeks called numbers that could be shown with this shape, square numbers.

This chart shows how to find square numbers by looking at number patterns.

Shape	Square Number	Add	Number Sentence
○	1	3	$1 = 1$
○○ ○○	4	5	$1 + 3 = 4$
○○○ ○○○ ○○○	9	7	$1 + 3 + 5 = 9$
○○○○ ○○○○ ○○○○ ○○○○	16		$1 + 3 + 5 + 7 = 16$

• What patterns do you see between square numbers?

• There are ten square numbers between 1 and 100. See if you can find them.

7

Lesser Number Game

Make a pack of number cards like these. Make the same number of sets as there are players.

Get each player to make a game board like this one.

hundred thousands	ten thousands	thousands	hundreds	tens	ones

How to play:

• Shuffle the cards and place them face down.

• Each player in turn takes a number card and places it in any open space on his or her game board. A number card cannot be moved after it is played.

• Continue playing until all the spaces on the game boards are filled.

• The player with the smallest number wins.

Odd and Even Maze

Here's an easy maze if you know the difference between odd and even numbers.

- Begin where it says 'Start'.

- Use your finger to trace a path through the maze. Or, make a copy and use a pencil. Never cross a line or go over the same place twice.

- Follow the odd numbers and be out in no time. Get mixed up with even numbers and you're trapped.

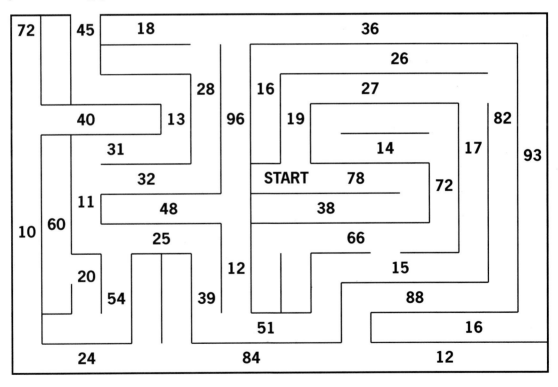

Make an odd or even maze of your own. Give your maze to a friend. See if your friend knows the difference between odd and even.

Guess the Number

Here's a number guessing game you and a friend can play together. The game takes some strategy. So put on your thinking cap.

You will need:

small index cards

a marker

How to play:

• Use index cards and a marker to make ten number cards. Arrange them in a row like this.

• Think of one of the numbers, but don't tell your partner.

• Your partner should try to work out your number by asking you 'yes' or 'no' questions.

• After each question, remove all the cards that are eliminated by the answer.

• Continue playing until the only card left is the one with your number on it.

Here is an example. Suppose you are thinking of the number 7.

Player: Is your number between 5 and 10?

You: Yes.

Remove cards 1 to 5 and the 10 card. Leave these cards.

Player: Is your number between 6 and 9?

You: Yes.

Remove the 6 and 9 cards. Leave these cards.

Player: Is your number an even number?

You: No.

Remove the 8 card. It is an even card. The 7 card is left.

• Think of some other questions you might have asked to get to the 7 card.

• Try playing the game with more cards. See how the game changes with the more cards you use.

• Play the game with more than two people.

• Make up your own rules about the kinds of questions that can be asked.

Tap Maze

This is an amazing maze. Follow the directions and find your way to the animal of your choice.

Here's what to do:

- Look at the pictures and select one of the animals.

- Use your finger to tap out the name of your animal letter by letter. The first tap should be on the 'Start' square.

- Jump from square to square as you name each letter. Be sure to follow the arrows.

- When you reach the last letter of your animal's name, you should be on its picture.

Try it several times to convince yourself it really works. Then try it out with your friends.

Make your own tap mazes:

- It's easy to make your own tap maze once you know the secret. The names in the maze must have consecutive numbers of letters, like this:

name	letters	name	letters
owl	3	penguin	7
deer	4	chipmunk	8
whale	5	porcupine	9
lizard	6	woodpecker	10

- Arrange the names and arrows so it will take the same number of taps to reach the name as there are letters in the name. Use the tap maze below as a model.

- Always begin with a 'Start' box and draw the first arrow to the name with the most letters.

- Then keep drawing arrows to names with increasing numbers of letters. Begin with the name with the fewest letters.

- You can place the names anywhere as long as the arrows point to the right ones.

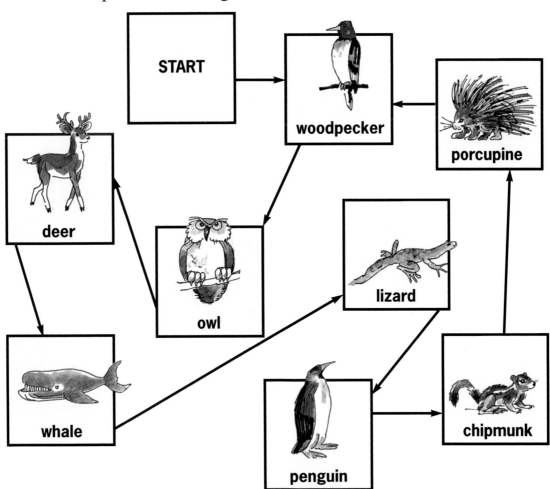

Place Value Toss Game

Here's a game for two to four players. All you need to know is a little about place value and regrouping.

You will need:

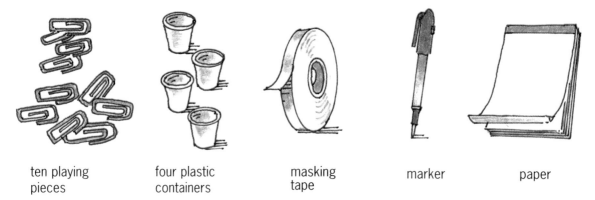

ten playing
pieces

four plastic
containers

masking
tape

marker

paper

To prepare:

• Use the masking tape to label the containers: thousands, hundreds, tens and ones.

• Arrange the containers in place value order on the floor or on a table.

• Get each player to make one or more score cards like the one on the next page.

14

How to play:

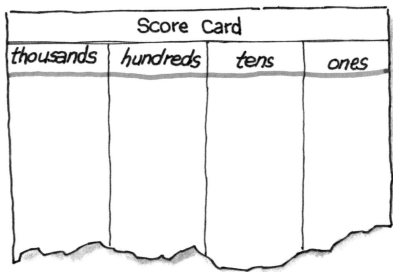

Score Card

thousands	hundreds	tens	ones

• Decide how far from the containers the players should be. Just over a metre works well.

• Each player is given ten game pieces to toss into the containers.

• Each player should record the number of pieces that land in each container. Then record the number in the squares on the score card. Remember, you may have to regroup.

• After every player has had a turn, compare score cards. The player with the largest number has won the game.

Try this:

• If it is too easy to get the playing pieces into the containers, move the players back.

• Try playing the game with fifteen or twenty playing pieces. This will increase the chances of regrouping when the scores are tallied up.

• Add ten thousands, hundred thousands, and millions containers. Change the score cards to match the containers.

Decimal Number Code

Somebody has messed up the decoder! You'll have to fix it. Arrange all the decimal numbers in consecutive order. Begin with the smallest number and end with the largest. Then use the fixed decoder to solve the riddles.

DECODER												
A	B	C	D	E	F	G	H	I	J	K	L	M
0.36	0.86	0.15	0.95	0.71	0.23	0.03	0.53	0.69	0.47	0.05	1.47	0.42
N	O	P	Q	R	S	T	U	V	W	X	Y	Z
1.9	0.08	1.76	0.82	0.12	0.28	0.99	0.62	1.22	0.56	0.01	0.75	0.39

What gets wetter the more it dries?

0.01   0.86—0.62—1.22—0.12—0.47

What did the greenhouse say to the doctor?

0.36   0.28—0.01—0.99—0.12
1.22—0.36—0.56—0.08—0.62—1.22
0.69—0.01—0.36—0.56—0.82

Why did the clock maker throw the clock out of the window?

0.28—0.12   1.22—0.01—0.56—0.86—0.12—0.08
0.86—0.62   0.82—0.12—0.12
0.86—0.36—0.53—0.12   0.15—0.47—1.76

Big Numbers

What's the biggest number you can think of?
Is it a thousand? A million? A trillion?

Numbers go on forever, and there are some
strange sounding names for some very large
numbers. Take a googol for example. It is a
1 followed by 100 zeros. Try writing it out.

million	1,000,000	undecillion	36 zeros
billion	1,000,000,000	duodecillion	39 zeros
trillion	1,000,000,000,000	tredecillion	42 zeros
quadrillion	1,000,000,000,000,000	quattuordecillion	45 zeros
quintillion	1,000,000,000,000,000,000	quindecillion	48 zeros
sextillion	1 followed by 21 zeros	sexdecillion	51 zeros
septillion	24 zeros	septendecillion	54 zeros
octillion	27 zeros	octodecillion	57 zeros
nonillion	30 zeros	novemdecillion	60 zeros
decillion	33 zeros	vigintillion	63 zeros

• Write some big numbers on a piece of paper
and ask a friend to name them. When your
friend gives up, impress everyone with the
answers.

• Here are some big number facts:

—your heart beats about 100,000 times a day
—about 700,000,000 people live in Africa
—the earth is about 4,500,000,000 years old
—there are about 200,000,000,000,000,000,000,000 stars

Make a book of big number facts. Look in
almanacs, encyclopedias, and *The Guinness Book
of World Records* for the facts you need.

Number Pair Picture Graphs

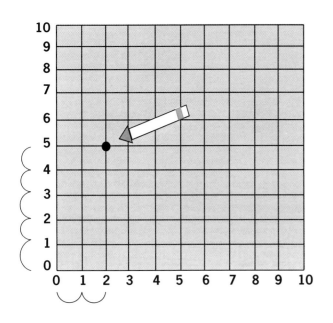

Number pairs are used to find points on a graph. Take the number pair (2,5) for example.

The first number in the pair matches the number along the bottom of the graph.

The second number in the pair matches the number on the side of the graph.

For the number pair (2,5), go across 2 and up 5. It's as simple as that.

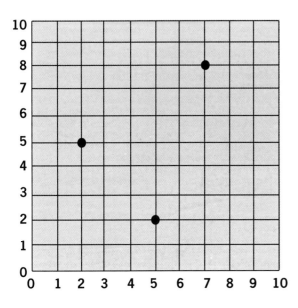

Using graph paper and number pairs you can make shapes and pictures.

First, use number pairs to find the points on the graph that will make a picture. Make a large dot on your graph paper where each point should be.

What number pairs would you use to tell where these points are?

Then connect the points to make a picture.

18

This triangle was made by connecting these points:

(2,5) —> (7,8) —> (5,2) —> (2,5)

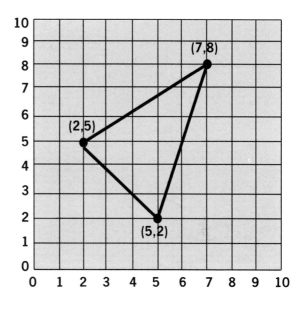

Use graph paper to draw the following shapes. Label your graphs with numbers 0 to 10 like this.

1. (2,9) —> (8,9) —> (8,7) —> (6,7) —> (6,2) —> (4,2) —> (4,7) —> (2,7) —> (2,9)

2. (4,8) —> (7,2) —> (1,6) —> (8,6) —> (2,2) —> (4,8)

3. (1,3) —> (4,6) —> (4,7) —> (5,6) —> (6,6) —> (8,4) —> (8,3) —> (5,3) —> (4,1) —> (1,3)

4. (1,2) —> (2,9) —> (1,9) —> (2,4) —> (2,2) —> (4,3) —> (3,4) —> (5,4) —> (6,2) —>(7,4) —> (7,0) —> (6,1) —> (8,3) —> (10,4) —> (8,4) —> (8,2) —> (10,2)

• Now try making a graph picture of your own. Give the number pairs to your friends and see who draws the best picture.

• Make a greeting card for someone special. Decorate the card with a number pair graph picture. Provide the graph and the number pairs, but not the picture. Your friend can join the dots to see your greeting.

19

Prime Numbers

About 2,000 years ago, a Greek mathematician named Eratosthenes developed a way to find prime numbers. His method is called the Sieve of Eratosthenes. You can use it to find the prime numbers from 1 to 100.

Here's what to do:

- Make a number chart like this one.

1	2	3	4	5	6	7	8	9	10
11	12	13	14	15	16	17	18	19	20
21	22	23	24	25	26	27	28	29	30
31	32	33	34	35	36	37	38	39	40
41	42	43	44	45	46	47	48	49	50
51	52	53	54	55	56	57	58	59	60
61	62	63	64	65	66	67	68	69	70
71	72	73	74	75	76	77	78	79	80
81	82	83	84	85	86	87	88	89	90
91	92	93	94	95	96	97	98	99	100

A prime number can only be divided by 1 and itself.

- Shade the 1. (Mathematicians don't think 1 is a prime number.)

1	2	3	4	5	6	7	8	9	10
11	12	13	14	15	16	17	18	19	20
21	22	23	24	25	26	27	28	29	30

- Two is the first prime number. Shade every second number after 2 – or, all the even numbers except 2.

- The second prime number is 3. Shade every third number after 3 – or, all multiples of 3 except 3. (Count the numbers that have already been shaded and those that haven't.)

1	2	3	4	5	6	7	8	9	10
11	12	13	14	15	16	17	18	19	20
21	22	23	24	25	26	27	28	29	30

- Five is the next prime number. Shade every fifth number after 5 – or, all multiples of 5 except 5.

1	2	3	4	5	6	7	8	9	10
11	12	13	14	15	16	17	18	19	20
21	22	23	24	25	26	27	28	29	30

- Seven is the next prime number. Shade every seventh number after 7. There will only be a few multiples of 7 that aren't already shaded.

At last you're finished. All the unshaded numbers on your chart are prime numbers. You should have twenty-five of them.

- What would be the next multiple to shade if your chart were larger?

- What do all your prime numbers except 2 have in common?

- Try making a larger number chart, say to 150. Find all the prime numbers using the Sieve of Eratosthenes. It's a lot of shading. You may want to take turns with a friend.

Binary Numbers

Look at these numbers. Can you find the pattern?

This kind of number pattern is called a binary number sequence. Each number is double the number before it.

- What is the next number in the pattern?

- What are the first ten numbers?

There is something very interesting about binary number sequences. By adding different combinations of the numbers, you can make many other numbers:

$$1 + 2 = 3$$
$$1 + 8 = 9$$
$$2 + 4 + 8 = 14$$
$$1 + 4 = 5$$
$$2 + 4 = 6$$
$$4 + 8 = 12$$
$$1 + 2 + 4 = 7$$
$$2 + 8 = 10$$
$$1 + 2 + 8 = 11$$

In fact, with the first five numbers, you can make all the numbers from 1 to 31. With the first ten numbers, you can make all the numbers up to 1,023!

- Make a chart like the one on the next page.
Try to make all the number combinations.

• Write 1's in the columns of the numbers you are using. Write 0's in the columns of the numbers you aren't using. The first few have been done for you.

• Add the number 16 in front of the number 8 at the top of the chart. Then extend your chart to 31.

Number	8	4	2	1
1				1
2			1	0
3			1	1
4		1	0	0
5		1	0	1
6		1	1	0
7				
8				
9				
10				
11				
12				
13				
14				
15				

As you filled in your chart you were writing binary numbers. You used only the digits 0 and 1. Normally you use the digits 0 to 9 to write numbers.

• Here's how you would usually write 10, and how you would write 10 as a binary number. How do the place values in the two systems differ?

tens	ones
1	0

eights	fours	twos	ones
1	0	1	0

So, what's so special about binary numbers? They're important because computers use them to do calculations.

Computers have only on and off switches – 1 is on and 0 is off. Computers use binary numbers because they are all made up of 1's and 0's.

Hot Dog Combinations

Almost everyone likes hot dogs. And one of the best parts about eating a hot dog is what you put on it.

Imagine that you have a choice of these three toppings. How many different combinations of toppings could you have with your hot dog?

It usually helps to make pictures when you are working out combinations.

That's right. There are seven combinations. Now comes the hard part. The more toppings, the more combinations you can have.

• Add onions to your choice of toppings to make four choices in all. How many combinations can you have now? What are they?

• Now add a pickle to make five choices. How many combinations?

• Now for the big time. Add brown sauce to make six choices. How many combinations?

Another Number Puzzle

Here's a number pattern that will make you think. But it's really quite simple.

See if you can figure out what the next line should be. If you do, go on to make two more lines. HINT: It helps to say the digits aloud.

1							
1	1						
2	1						
1	2	1	1				
1	1	1	2	2	1		
3	1	2	2	1	1		
1	3	1	1	2	2	2	1

Some Wordy Puzzles

You have 8 litres of milk. But all you need is 1 litre. All you have at hand is a 3-litre and a 5-litre jug. How can you get the litre you need?

There are 8 sons in a family. Each one of them has 1 sister. How many people are in the family?

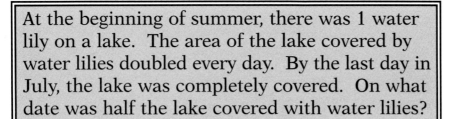

At the beginning of summer, there was 1 water lily on a lake. The area of the lake covered by water lilies doubled every day. By the last day in July, the lake was completely covered. On what date was half the lake covered with water lilies?

Prime Dot-to-Dot

Remember prime numbers? If not, take a look at pages 20–21. Then try your hand at this dot-to-dot picture.

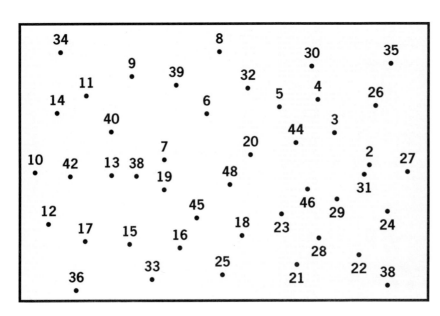

Use tracing paper or make a copy. Then connect each prime number to the next highest prime number.

Odd and Even Tic-Tac-Toe

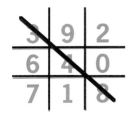

Try this twist on an old game. Instead of O's and X's, one player uses the odd numbers 1, 3, 5, 7 and 9. The other player uses 0 and the even numbers 2, 4, 6 and 8.

The player with the odd numbers goes first. Each number can only be used once.

The winner is the player who can write a number that gives a sum of 15 for any row, column or diagonal.

Answers

Pages 4/5 Numbers Past and Present
The Arabic numbers for the Roman numerals on the clock are:

I = 1; II = 2; III = 3; IV = 4; V = 5; VI = 6; VII = 7; VIII = 8; IX = 9; X = 10; XI = 11; XII = 12.

The hands on the clock are pointing to 12 and 4.
The time is 4 o'clock.

1. 14   2. 54   3. 102   4. 13   5. 17
6. 16   7. 52   8. 110   9. 27   10. 51
11. 150 12. 210

6/7 Number Shapes
The next triangular number is 10. It looks like this.

Removing two rows leaves the triangular number 3. It looks like this.

To find triangular numbers, start at 1 and keep adding the next number.

The fifteen triangular numbers from 1 to 120 are:

1, 3, 6, 10, 15, 21, 28, 36, 45, 55, 66, 78, 91, 105, 120

The number shown is 9. The shape it makes is a square.

The next biggest square number is 16. It looks like this.

To find square numbers, start at 1 and keep adding the next odd number.

The ten square numbers from 1 to 100 are:

1, 4, 9, 16, 25, 36, 49, 64, 81, 100

8 Lesser Number Game
No answers.

9 Odd and Even Maze

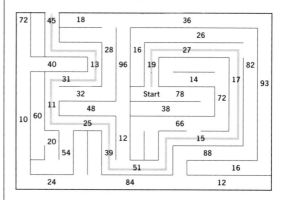

10/11 Guess the Number
No answers.

12/13 Tap Maze
No answers.

14/15 Place Value Toss Game
No answers.

Answers

16 Decimal Number Code

Your decoder should look like this:

A	B	C	D	E	F	G	H	I	J	K	L	M
0.01	0.03	0.05	0.08	0.12	0.15	0.23	0.28	0.36	0.39	0.42	0.47	0.53

N	O	P	Q	R	S	T	U	V	W	X	Y	Z
0.56	0.62	0.69	0.71	0.75	0.82	0.86	0.95	0.99	1.22	1.47	1.76	1.9

What gets wetter the more it dries?

A towel.

What did the greenhouse say to the doctor?

I have window pains.

Why did the clock maker throw the clock out of the window?

He wanted to see time fly.

17 Big Numbers

No answers.

18/19 Number Pair Picture Graphs

The pairs are (5,2), (2,5), and (7,8).

1.

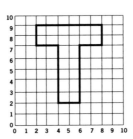

2.

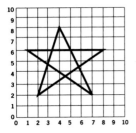

3.

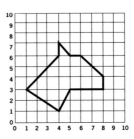

4.

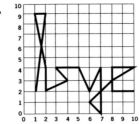

20/21 Prime Numbers

The twenty-five unshaded prime numbers on your chart should be: 2, 3, 5, 7, 11, 13, 17, 19, 23, 29, 31, 37, 41, 43, 47, 53, 59, 61, 67, 71, 73, 79, 83, 89, 97.

The next multiple to shade if your chart were larger would be 11.

All your prime numbers except 2 are odd numbers.

22/23 Binary Numbers

The next number in the pattern is 32.

The first ten numbers in the pattern are:

1, 2, 4, 8, 16, 32, 64, 128, 256, 512

Your chart should look like this:

Numbers	16	8	4	2	1
1					1
2				1	0
3				1	1
4			1	0	0
5			1	0	1
6			1	1	0
7			1	1	1
8		1	0	0	0
9		1	0	0	1
10		1	0	1	0
11		1	0	1	1
12		1	1	0	0
13		1	1	0	1
14		1	1	1	0
15		1	1	1	1
16	1	0	0	0	0
17	1	0	0	0	1
18	1	0	0	1	0
19	1	0	0	1	1
20	1	0	1	0	0
21	1	0	1	0	1
22	1	0	1	1	0
23	1	0	1	1	1
24	1	1	0	0	0
25	1	1	0	0	1
26	1	1	0	1	0
27	1	1	0	1	1
28	1	1	1	0	0
29	1	1	1	0	1
30	1	1	1	1	0
31	1	1	1	1	1

In the usual way you write numbers, the place values are ones, tens, hundreds, and so on. In the binary number system the place values are ones, twos, fours, eights and so on.

24 Hot Dog Combinations

With four toppings there are fifteen combinations:

ketchup—**ketchup**/mustard—**ketchup**/relish—**ketchup**/onions—**ketchup**/mustard/relish—**ketchup**/mustard/onions—**ketchup**/relish/onions—**ketchup**/mustard/relish/onions—**mustard**—**mustard**/relish—**mustard**/onions—**mustard**/relish/onions—**relish**—**relish**/onions—**onions**

With five toppings there are thirty-one combinations. All the ones above plus these:

ketchup/pickle—**ketchup**/mustard/pickle—**ketchup**/onions/pickle—**ketchup**/relish/pickle—**ketchup**/mustard/onions/pickle—**ketchup**/mustard/relish/pickle—**ketchup**/onions/relish/pickle—**ketchup**/mustard/onions/relish/pickle—**mustard**/pickle—**mustard**/onions/pickle—**mustard**/relish/pickle—**mustard**/onions/relish/pickle—**onions**/pickle—**onions**/relish/pickle—**relish**/pickle—**pickle**

With six toppings there are sixty-three combinations. All the ones for four and five toppings plus these:

sauce—**sauce**/ketchup—**sauce**/mustard—**sauce**/onions—**sauce**/relish—**sauce**/pickle—**sauce**/ketchup/mustard—**sauce**/ketchup/onions—**sauce**/ketchup/relish—**sauce**/ketchup/pickle—**sauce**/mustard/onions—**sauce**/mustard/relish—**sauce**/mustard/pickle—**sauce**/onions/relish—**sauce**/onions/pickle—**sauce**/relish/pickle—**sauce**/ketchup/mustard/onions—**sauce**/ketchup/mustard/relish—**sauce**/ketchup/mustard/pickle—**sauce**/ketchup/onions/relish—**sauce**/ketchup/onions/pickle—**sauce**/ketchup/relish/pickle—**sauce**/mustard/onions/relish—

Answers

sauce/mustard/onions/pickle—**sauce**/ mustard/relish/pickle—**sauce**/onions/ relish/pickle—**sauce**/ketchup/mustard/ onions/relish—**sauce**/ketchup/mustard/ onions/pickle—**sauce**/ketchup/ mustard/relish/pickle—**sauce**/ketchup/ onions/relish/pickle—**sauce**/ mustard/ onions/relish/pickle—**sauce**/ketchup/ mustard/onions/relish/pickle

25 Another Number Puzzle

Each new line counts the digits in the previous line. Like this:

line 2 counts line one: one 1

line 3 counts line two: two 1s

line 4 counts line 3: one 2, one 1

line 5 counts line 4: one 1, one 2, two 1s

line 6 counts line 5: three 1s, two 2s, one 1

line 7 counts line 6: one 3, one 1, two 2s, two 1s

Continuing in the same way, the next three lines are:

1113213211   31131211131221
13211311123113112211

Some Wordy Puzzles

Fill the 3-litre jug and pour it into the 5-litre jug. Fill the 3-litre jug again and use it to fill the same 5-litre jug to the top. One litre of milk remains in the 3-litre jug.

The family consists of 11 people: 8 sons, the mother, the father, and 1 daughter.

Remember, the area of the lake covered doubles everyday. The lake will be half covered on July 30, since July has 31 days. Double a half and you get a whole.

26 Prime Dot-to-Dot

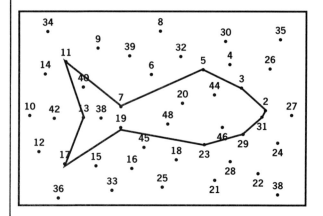

Odd and Even Tic-Tac-Toe

No answers.

Glossary

binary number A number with a base of 2 that is written with the digits 0 and 1. For example: The binary number for the number 10 is written 1010.

binary sequence A sequence of numbers in which each number is double the number before it. For example: 1, 2, 4, 8, 16, 32.

consecutive Following one after the other in some kind of order or sequence.

decimal number A number with a base of 10.

digits The symbols used to write numerals: 0, 1, 2, 3, 4, 5, 6, 7, 8 and 9.

even number A whole number that ends in 0, 2, 4, 6 or 8. A multiple of two.

number pairs Pairs of numbers used to locate points on a graph. Coordinates.

odd number A whole number that ends in 1, 3, 5, 7 or 9. Not a multiple of two.

place value The value given to the place where a digit occurs in a number.

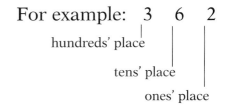

For example: 3   6   2
hundreds' place
tens' place
ones' place

prime number A number that has only two factors – itself and 1.

square A rectangle with all four sides straight and the same length.

triangle A figure with three straight sides.

Index